Great African Americans

Satchel Paige

THE BEST ARM IN BASEBALL

Revised Edition

Patricia and Fredrick McKissack

Series Consultant
Dr. Russell L. Adams, Chairman
Department of Afro-American Studies, Howard University

Enslow Publishers, Inc.

40 Industrial Road   PO Box 38
Box 398   Aldershot
Berkeley Heights, NJ 07922   Hants GU12 6BP
USA   UK

http://www.enslow.com

To Elizabeth and Gilbert Merritt

Revised edition of *Satchel Paige: The Best Arm in Baseball* © 1992

Library of Congress Cataloging-in-Publication Data

McKissack, Pat, 1944–
    Satchel Paige : the best arm in baseball / Patricia and Fredrick McKissack.— Rev. ed.
        p. cm. — (Great African Americans)
    Includes index.
    ISBN 0–7660–1699–4
    1. Paige, Leroy, 1906–1982—Juvenile literature. 2. Baseball players—United States—Biography—
Juvenile literature. 3. African American baseball players—Biography—Juvenile literature. [1. Paige,
Leroy, 1906–1982. 2. Baseball players. 3. African Americans—Biography.] I. McKissack, Fredrick.
II. Title. III. Series.
    GV865.P3 M36   2001
    796.357'092—dc21
                                                                          00–012421

Printed in the United States of America

10 9 8 7 6 5 4 3

To Our Readers
We have done our best to make sure all Internet Addresses in this book were active and appropriate when we went to press. However, the author and the publisher have no control over and assume no liability for the material available on those Internet sites or on other Web sites they may link to. Any comments or suggestions can be sent by e-mail to comments@enslow.com or to the address on the back cover.

Every effort has been made to locate all copyright holders of materials used in this book. If any errors or omissions have occurred, corrections will be made in future editions of this book.

Table of Contents

Leroy (Satchel) Paige
July 7, 1906–June 8, 1982

CHAPTER 1

Living in a Shotgun

When Satchel Paige was born, he was named Leroy Paige. Leroy grew up in a large family. He had ten brothers and sisters. His parents worked very, very hard. His father earned money as a gardener. His mother washed and ironed clothes for money. But the family was still poor.

The Paiges lived in a small house on Franklin Street in Mobile, Alabama. It was called a shotgun house. There were four rooms, one behind the other. "A straight shot from the front door to the back," Satchel said.

When Leroy was seven years old, he earned money at the train station. He carried travelers' bags, sometimes called satchels, for money. He carried so many at one time, his friends said

When Satchel was a child, he lived in a shotgun house like these in Mobile, Alabama.

Downtown Mobile in the early 1900s.

he was a "satchel tree." Pretty soon he was just called Satchel.

When he wasn't working, Satchel liked to throw things. It was fun hitting trees and cans with rocks. He became good at it. First, he took aim. Then he threw the rock. Zap! He hit the mark almost every time.

7

CHAPTER 2

Mount Meigs, Alabama

Satchel didn't like school. So he didn't go very often. Then he was caught stealing toys. In 1918, when Satchel was twelve years old, a judge sent him to reform school at the Industrial School for Negro Children at Mount Meigs, Alabama. He stayed there until he was seventeen.

"It was the best thing that happened to me,"

8

Years ago in the South, black teams were not allowed to play against white teams. These ballplayers were from Morris Brown College in Atlanta, Georgia.

Satchel said later. "I was running around with the wrong crowd."

At Mount Meigs, he stopped throwing rocks and learned how to throw a baseball on the school baseball team. That was the beginning.

Satchel Paige would still be throwing baseballs thirty years later. His pitching arm would make him a star.

When Satchel left Mount Meigs he was about 6 feet 3½ inches tall. He weighed 140 pounds. "I was so tall and thin everybody called me 'The Crane,'" he said.

Baseball great Babe Ruth, left, was already famous by the time Satchel started to play. Years later Satchel would be called "the Babe Ruth of the Negro Leagues."

Satchel wanted to play baseball, so he joined the Mobile Tigers. All the ballplayers were black. Wilson Paige, one of Satchel's brothers, played for the Tigers, too. Satchel was the team's star pitcher.

CHAPTER 3

The Traveling Man

i n the 1920s, the United States was segregated. There were laws that kept blacks and whites from going to school together. They could not live in the same neighborhoods. And they could not play professional sports in the same leagues. African Americans played baseball in the "Negro Leagues."

Being a Negro League ballplayer wasn't easy. The team traveled in old cars and run-down buses. They weren't welcome in most hotels

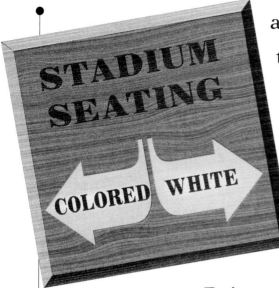

In the 1920s, laws kept blacks and whites apart—even at baseball games.

and restaurants. Many times the team had to sleep on the ballpark benches.

White fans came to see the black teams play. Sometimes those fans shouted unkind things to the black players. But when they saw Satchel Paige pitch, they cheered. His best pitch was the fast ball. He called it his "bee ball," because it hummed like a bee. He also threw a hard breaking curve ball and a fast slider.

In 1926, he joined the Chattanooga Black Lookouts. He earned $50 a month. "Big money for me then," Satchel said. But he was restless. He moved from team to team. From 1926 to 1934, Satchel Paige pitched for teams in Birmingham, Alabama, and Cleveland, Ohio. Satchel proved how

Satchel was a great pitcher. But he was also a good bunter. Here he is ready to bunt.

good he was with the Pittsburgh Crawfords between 1931 and 1934. Satchel helped the Crawfords win the Negro National League title in 1933.

Baseball season in the Negro Leagues attracted huge crowds. Parades and other special events added to the excitement.

During off-seasons, Satchel played for teams in the Caribbean, Mexico, and South America. He was known as a "traveling man."

On October 26, 1934, Satchel married Janet Howard. They did not live together very much. Satchel liked to travel. He just could not settle down. Soon the marriage ended.

Now Satchel was getting older. Some people thought his pitching arm had burned out. The Kansas

Coming !
Famous Colored Teams

The Base Ball Fans here are in a frenzy of enthusiasm over the Opening Games of the Colored Base Ball Teams at League Park, beginning Saturday, April 30th. The Famous "A. B. C's." of Indianapolis will cross bats with the renowned "Cuban Stars". Both teams are "Way Out In the Front" in the Base Ball World. Col. I. C. Taylor of Indianapolis, will be here in person, and all who know "I. C." realize that he always stands for the best there is in America's Great National game. During the absence of the Reds this season Colored Teams have games scheduled. Best of Order. , Best of Accomodations. Popular Prices! DON'T FORGET—The coming games take place Saturday, April 30th, Sunday, Monday, Tuesday and Wednesday, May 1st to 4th.

Crowds loved to see Satchel Paige, above, because he played great baseball and entertained audiences at the same time. Here, the Monarchs played the New York Cuban Stars in Yankee Stadium in New York.

City Monarchs signed him to a contract anyway. The Monarchs were smart. Satchel had many more seasons left to pitch.

**Monarch pitcher Satchel Paige smiles from the dugout
during this game in 1942.**

CHAPTER 4

The Monarch Years

Between 1939 and 1942, the Monarchs won the Negro American League championship every year. Satchel was a big part of it. The Monarchs beat the Homestead Grays and won the Negro World Series in 1942. Satchel pitched the winning game. He was older now, but he was as good as ever.

Satchel did not make a whole lot of money. But he made more than most black ballplayers did in the 1940s. If Satchel had been white, he would have

Satchel gave
nicknames
to his
pitches. Some
famous ones
were the
"hesitation
pitch,"
"wobbly
ball," "jump
ball," and
"trouble
ball."

pitched for one of the major league teams. But he could play only in the Negro Leagues.

Satchel was one of the best pitchers who ever played the game. And he was the first to say it! Satchel loved to brag as much as he liked to make people laugh. Satchel said and did funny things on and off the baseball field. One of his most famous sayings was, "Don't look back. Something might be gaining on you."

Satchel spent a lot of money, too. He went back to visit his mother in Mobile. She was still living in the same small shotgun house. One day he took her out for a ride. He showed her a large house and asked her if she liked it. She said it was too big.

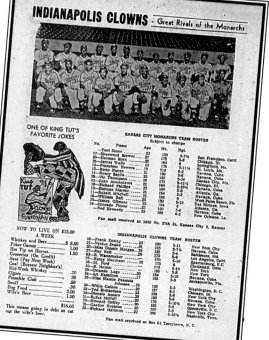

The Monarchs often played the Indianapolis Clowns.

Satchel said it was hers. He had already bought it for her. At last, he moved his mother out of the shotgun shack.

Satchel, right, with pitching star Dizzy Dean, center, and Cecil Davis. In some very special games, top black players would play against top white players.

Satchel's girlfriend, Lahoma Brown, wanted him to spend his money wisely. She talked him into buying a large home in Kansas City. On October 12, 1947, they were married in Hays, Kansas.

Satchel signs copies of *Maybe I'll Pitch Forever*, the book he wrote about his life.

CHAPTER 5

If He Were White

In 1947, Jackie Robinson was chosen as the first black player to start in the all-white National League. He played for the Brooklyn Dodgers.

Satchel was hurt that he had not been the first black player in the National League. He had worked long and hard for the chance to be that player. But a lot of people thought he was too old.

Satchel finally got his chance in the majors on July 9, 1948. He signed up with the Cleveland Indians. That made him the first black pitcher in the American League. At forty-two years old, he was also the oldest rookie.

Jackie Robinson, right, was the first black man to play in the all-white major leagues.

Satchel won six games and lost one during his first season. His team won the American League championship. They also won the 1948 World Series against the Boston Braves.

Satchel got to pitch only one inning in the World Series. It was enough for him. He said, ". . . it felt great!" Satchel was very proud. Even at his age, he could still throw a baseball hard, fast, and straight.

Satchel retired after the 1949 season. But not for long. He played whenever he could for many more years. Finally, he became a coach for the Atlanta Braves. And in 1968, he really did retire.

In the early days, Negro League teams traveled by car or bus. By the 1950s, they used airplanes. Here, Satchel looks ready for takeoff.

Satchel talks with Bill Veeck, right, who invited him to pitch for the Cleveland Indians in 1948 and the St. Louis Browns in 1951.

All his life, Satchel had heard: "We sure could use a pitcher like you. If you were white." But he was never bitter. "I don't look back," he said often.

Satchel won many honors for his work in baseball on and off the field. His greatest honor

This statue of Satchel Paige is in the Negro Leagues Baseball Museum in Kansas City, Missouri.

came in August 1971. Leroy "Satchel" Paige was accepted into the Baseball Hall of Fame.

Most great Negro League baseball players were part of their own Hall of Fame. They were still segregated. Satchel Paige was a great pitcher. He was placed alongside other great major league players like Babe Ruth and Jackie Robinson. For the first time, nobody said, "If he were only white." His skin color didn't matter.

Satchel lived in Kansas City with Lahoma for the rest of his life. He died on June 8, 1982.

timeLiNe

1906 ~ Leroy "Satchel" Paige is born on July 7.

1918 ~ Is sent to reform school.

1924 ~ Begins his baseball career with the Mobile Tigers, a semipro team.

1926 ~ Begins playing for a variety of Negro League teams.

1930s & 1940s ~ Takes part in "barnstorming" tours around the country, often playing in exhibition games against top major league stars. Pitches in more than 2,000 games.

1939 ~ Signs with the Kansas City Monarchs.

1948 ~ Becomes the first black pitcher to join the American League. Pitches for the Cleveland Indians in the World Series.

1968 ~ Retires from baseball.

1971 ~ Is elected to the Baseball Hall of Fame.

1982 ~ Dies on June 8.

WORDS TO KNOW

American League—One of two groups of major league teams that play among themselves to win a pennant. The pennant winner plays the National League pennant winner in the World Series.

Baseball Hall of Fame—A special place where baseball players are honored for their careers.

major league—A group of professional baseball teams that play against each other for championships.

National League—One of two groups of major league teams that play among themselves to win a pennant. The pennant winner plays the American League pennant winner in the World Series.

Negro—A word that was used for African Americans at one time. It is not used much any more.

Negro Leagues—A group of all-black baseball teams that played only against each other.

Negro World Series—The top team in the Negro National League played the top team in the Negro American League for the championship.

WORDS TO KNOW

reform school—A special school where children who get into trouble with the law are sent.

retire—To stop working permanently at a regular job or profession.

satchel—An old name for a traveling bag that usually had a shoulder strap.

segregated—Separated from, apart. At one time, the United States had separate schools for blacks and whites. The races could not work together or share public accommodations, like hotels, restaurants, and rest rooms.

shotgun house—A house where all the rooms are placed one behind the other. If you opened up all the doors in the house, you could shoot a shotgun through the front door and the shot would come out the back door without going through any walls.

Learn more about Leroy (Satchel) Paige

Books

Cline-Ransome, Lesa. *Satchel Paige*. New York: Simon & Schuster, 2000.

Macht, Norman L. *Satchel Paige*. Broomall, Pa.: Chelsea House Publishers, 1991.

Internet Addresses

Negro Leagues Baseball Museum
<http://www.nlbm.com>

Official Web site of Satchel Paige
<http://www.cmgww.com/baseball/paige/index.html>

Negro Leagues Players in National Baseball Hall of Fame
<http://www.blackbaseball.com/players/index.htm>

index